S0-BTD-157

09/'24
STRAND PRICE
$ 5.00

For Susan,

My best wishes,

Bettie Sellers

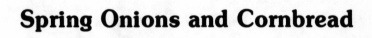

Spring Onions and Cornbread

Also by Bettie M. Sellers

Westward from Bald Mountain

SPRING ONIONS
and
CORNBREAD

By Bettie M. Sellers

PELICAN PUBLISHING COMPANY
GRETNA 1978

Copyright © 1978
By Bettie M. Sellers
All rights reserved

Library of Congress Cataloging in Publication Data

Sellers, Bettie M.
  Spring onions and cornbread

  I. Title.
PS3569.E5745S6   811'.5'4   77-27036
ISBN: 0-88289-179-0

Manufactured in the United States of America

Published by Pelican Publishing Company, Inc.
630 Burmaster Street, Gretna, Louisiana 70053

Cover design by David Sellers

For Bill, Guinn, and Eddie
who grew up at Shoal Creek
and
In loving memory of George
who died there

Spring Onions and Cornbread

SIDE BY SIDE ON THE TABLE SAT

I stopped today by Highway 16,
ate spring onions, crisp and hot,
from Jean's garden.
Her grandson rubbed his chin
against my boots
and remembered brown eyes begged
another round—"This little piggie went
to market" on bare pink toes.
His tall father grinned down at me:
"You gonna put Mama in your book?"
(as though she hadn't been there
since the first grade,
reciting THE GINGHAM DOG AND THE CALICO CAT
in a blue silk dress,
smocked, with little pink roses
on the yoke.)

GYPSIES AND WATER MOCCASINS

Two things we feared!
snakes to strike bare feet,
and the gypsies camped in ragged caravans
at Double Sewers where Shoal Creek
ran deep under Highway 16.
A moccasin bit Eula Dragg
(she did my mama's washing,
brought it home tied in a sheet
balanced on her head).
For twenty years, the misery in her leg
had told of rain long before the thunder spoke.
"I shoulda took that ol' snake to ol' Ida,
she woulda conjured the pain away."
From our porch we could see the lights
criss-crossing the leaning cabin
where Old Ida cast her spells.
Folks came in big cars,
big cars from Griffin and Barnesville—
Mag said they came to get spells for enemies,
and love potions—but Old Ida had the evil eye, too.
She cursed Mag's man, and he was gone.
Come dawn, the devil flapping at her window,
heavy like a Yellow Hammer nailing on the rooftree.
The gypsies came with dog days in July,
roaming Highway 16 for unguarded horses
and unwary children.

Mama said they sold you into white slavery
(whatever that was)
and their black iron cooking pots bubbled
greasy with stews of somebody's chickens
charmed from the henhouse on a moonless night.
I killed my first snake,
slithering in our swimming hole
dammed up at Double Sewers,
one July day when the gypsies had gone.

BY SHOAL CREEK

The big poplar down in the pasture
was my hiding place.
The limbs branched wide
in a secluded perch leafed away
from tugging hands that begged
another game of tag or mumblety-peg.
High, high above the rumble of pigs,
the ruminating low of cows,
it overlooked a universe beyond
the farm's green barbed-wire edge.
I carried Roland there
and heard him blow his mighty horn
loud across Shoal Creek
to Rouncesvalles and the highest Pyrenees.
Ganelon whispered, treacherous
in the quivering leaves—
moments when the earth fell suddenly too quiet,
coiled like a copperhead asleep in the sun.
Then Charlemagne strode tall across the pasture,
driving Bess and Lou home for milking time.
Their metal bells clanked comforting as shining mail,
ringing the creekbank safe again
in the summer afternoon.

THAT AWFUL SUMMER WHEN I WAS TWELVE

Summer noons, Bodiddly and the other hands
came in from the fields to eat greens and fatback
with thick squares of cornbread
in the deep shade behind the house.
The air under the pecan trees was warm and rank
with sweat-smelling bodies,
new-plowed earth,
and mules munching dusty oats.
Isaiah he was (after the prophet),
but my dad called him Bodiddly
from the time he was a shaver
dropping corn behind his daddy's plow.
Lean as a fence rail,
Bo was the Step-n-Fetchit of Spalding County—
buck-dancing barefoot on the summer grass
to "Li'l Liza Jane" and "Shady Grove,"
he entertained our nooning.
And his stories—shivery delights:
hants and goblins a-tapping of your shoulder
if you ventured in the deep pine woods;
foxfire moons fleeting ghostly
above the midnight river swamps.
Than one dark August day,
my grandmother came to visit!
"Bettie Crosby, you come in this house this minute!
You are too big to fool around with the hands.
It's just not nice!"

On the front steps, I cried a spate of tears,
blew my nose on my hateful skirt,
and cursed my brothers
munching the cornbread of freedom
with Bodiddly under a pecan tree.

STILL LIFE WITH PENNY CANDY

C. M. drove the No. 2 bus from the county line
to Griffin and went back home to run the store
where the dirt road to Mt. Zion Campground
crossed Highway 16. The train tracks
were overgrown with weeds even then,
and the stationhouse sagged heavy with Crowder's hay.
Now, the wood stove in the back of C. M.'s store
is gone, and Mr. Sampson waiting for someone
to play checkers on an upturned nail keg.
The penny candy case and big round lemony cookies
two cents a piece have disappeared with Ettie Jones
who caught the bus at the store and snatched
my cap because she could.
I never stood up to her but once—
pushed beyond endurance, I snatched a handful
of red hair out as Ettie stepped down laughing
from the No. 2 bus.

RED BADGE

She worked in Mama's kitchen
scrubbing pots and floors—
Old Nora in her layers
of cast-off garments,
strange Joseph's coat
of many ragged lengths.
Her family, a brood of "granchirren"
with mouths like hungry birds
for the old woman to feed.
Her yard, sagging doorstep and all,
a profusion of tall red cockscomb,
in clustered patterns
on the broom-clean earth.

WHITE OAK MAKES THE BEST BASKETS

"Eighty-five, ninety, ninety-five, a hundred,
who ain't ready, holler out I!"
Becky's behind the feedroom door,
her flowerdy dresstail sticking out through the crack.
Sister's under the cotton basket in the shed,
curled up like a hound asleep in the shade.

White oak makes the best baskets,
big ones for cotton and little ones for eggs,
and one for Mama to bring the washing
in off the line on Mondays.
Old Mr. Barfield made our baskets,
split out logs to strips
not half a finger's thickness
and soaked them limber in the watering trough
(the mules didn't seem to mind
the faint sweet taste of white oak sap).
"You have to work 'em wet," he said,
"they stiffen up when they dry.
This here basket'll last a hunnert years
if'n you treat it right."
And the splinter-scarred fingers
moved in and out with long splits of oak,
weaving a basket just big enough to hide under.

THE DEVIL'S DARNING NEEDLES

Dragon flies and "snake doctors" darted
green gauze wings over rainbow-stained pools
hoof deep in the mud of the barnyard.
Nora said they would sew up our ears
if we didn't mind what she said.
The "devil's darning needles" she called them,
her superstitions fearsome and real
as her dark mistrust of Dr. Frye
who spanked life into three of us
in the back room at Shoal Creek.
Barely four when George was born,
Bill trudged across the pasture
to fetch Nora to get Mama "night-gowned
and kivered up" before the doctor came.
Unwilling to leave his mama with that man
whose black bag brought shots and babies,
Bill ran away from Nora,
but pulled up short, jerked into
an everlasting horror of *all* doctors:
"Don' you go back in dat house, boy,
dat doctor sew up bof yo ears wif his needle—
jus lak dat ol' snake doctor do."

I'LL CUT OFF THEIR HEADS WITH A CARVING KNIFE

My aunt Alma had picnics
down in the pasture
on hot summer afternoons.
It was after the pimento cheese
and lemonade that Dorothy
had the brilliant idea!
Let's catch lightning bugs.
A quart jar full
(the lemonade being all gone).
Then the idea of the century hit
Becky and Sue:
Let's put 'em all down Bettie's back!
I hated bugs then;
I hate bugs now.
And I still have a faint urge to kill
somebody
when fireflies chase each other
up and down the pasture
like so many stars
having a mid-summer picnic.

CLEAN RAGS AND KEROSENE

Spring came to the creek
with the first stumped toe of March.
Throbbing in a clean rag
soaked in kerosene,
it was our badge of freedom
from winter's worn-down shoes.
With shoes, we shucked our hated underwear,
ordered white from Sears' fall catalogue
and boiled grey in the washpot
by Eula Dragg on Mondays.
Tight shoes and union suits
from late October to my birthday,
the last week in March.
(Bill got watermelon and roasting ears
for his birthday in mid-July).
One spring we all had the seven-year-itch,
passed around at school by the Bryant kids.
Greased with sulfur and lard every day
for a week, we stayed home
stinking worse than the pig pen
in a long wet spell.
Cured, we built a fire behind the barn
and offered up our underwear
with pine boughs
and yellow smoke rising.

CIGAR BANDS AND TOBACCO TAGS

I. TOBACCO TAGS

Small boys jostling.
Red tops spinning,
dancing in an earth-drawn ring.
"Mine, It's mine!
Out of the ring, it's mine!"
Sharp metal tips darting,
nudging bright tobacco tags
saved from Grandpa's chewing plugs.
Mules and circles, bulls and parallelograms
cut from tin and painted red or brown.
"Trade you five 'Brown's Mule'
for one 'Snaps.' "
"Naw, how about three 'Bull of the Woods'
for one 'Favorite'?"
Value seriously appraised,
set by the old laws of supply and demand—
coin of the realm,
counted from a draw-stringed tobacco sack.

II. BIRD CARDS

Folks around Shoal Creek used ARM AND HAMMER
for just about everything;
toothpaste, indigestion, baking, cleaning.
And the kids collected 1½ x 3-inch cards,
dusted off the soda
to read about Horned Grebes and their habitat,
how many eggs and what color.
Cockatoos and Kiwis we knew so well, it would
have been no surprise to meet one in the feather.
You could tote ten bird cards nicely
in a tobacco sack.
"Give ya two Bald Eagles for one Tufted Titmouse."
"OK, if you'll swap me a Yellow Hammer
for three Bluebirds."

III. AND CIGAR BANDS

Dad bought his cigars
in a wooden box (great for storing things)—
but woe betide the unfortunate scamp
who dared to snitch the bands
and let the air dry out the aromatic rolls.
It was daily ceremony.
Prying up the tiny nail that held the lid,
choosing just the right cigar,
bestowing the golden circle
upon the favored one.
Golden paper rings and mock weddings performed
in the back pasture. Housekeeping started
in square rooms laid off
with rows and rows of smooth creek stones.

LANEY

"Honey, you go up the hill—
see if Laney's all right."
I'm too little to be told why.
Not too little to wade across the creek
and climb the long rocky hill
to Laney's house.
Tom's not there now—
a white-gowned ghost
runs through the empty house,
bare feet soundless
on the sand-scrubbed pine boards.
The baby's crib is gone—
up in the attic, maybe,
and the bib I made,
embroidered with a pink butterfly.
I don't go to Laney's any more.
They nailed boards over all the windows,
and I heard Mama telling Eula Dragg
that Laney drank a whole bottle of Lysol
in a phone booth on Main St.

BRAVE COUNTRY GIRL

Each spring the Doziers came
with their rat-killing dog,
Trixie, I think her name was—
not much bigger than a rat herself.
The men tore up the planks
of the corncrib floor
and cheered Trixie,
shaking rats to death
between her sharp terrier teeth.
I covered my ears and hid
behind a peach tree.

I caught a mouse once,
by the tip of his tail
in a trap.
It was so frightened,
I let it go.
And Dad brought me a rooster
when supper was scarce—
I stood all morning,
ax in hand;
we had pork and beans
for supper.

THE DAY DICK AND JANE BIT THE DUST

I must have been ten the spring
a traveling troupe came to tread
the creaking boards at Orrs Elementary.
"The Merchant of Venice" it was—
and the country girl soared off,
brief in hand, into a grease-paint world.
No more a cowboy aiming stick rifles
at the wily Sioux in the plum thicket
behind the school, I glided down dirt paths
to Belmont and beyond, pleading my case
with maidenly conviction
or walking as became a queen
on the arm of my lord Bassanio.
It dropped again, that gentle rain,
when my cousin, grown-up with his newest
hobby, covered the complete plays
in white leather for my birthday.
Portia had come to our house to stay,
daily expounding the quality of mercy
to Bess and Lou in the pasture
or the crayfish stirring up the mud
in the bottom of Shoal Creek.

FIRE AT NIGHT

Country fires don't leave much:
a chimney's stacked rocks
stronger than Prometheus' gift,
and the brass bedstead twisted
in a grotesque caricature
of the lives conceived and born
from its creaking springs.
The Walker's house burned one dark night.
Their children were grown and gone,
but she gave me a birthday party
when I was twelve.
We ran across the fields,
drawn by the glow. Nothing was left
but the bed where we laid our coats,
and the fieldstone hearth where we toasted
marshmallows and pinned the tail on the donkey.

A POOR EXCUSE FOR A GIRLCHILD

Left-handed and awkward . . . dirty fingers
that could shinny up trees as good as the boys,
but left disgraceful smudges on the linen teacloth:
GOD BLESS OUR HOME (cross-stitched)
under a ragged pink butterfly.
"Take that stitch out, child, and don't squirm so."
For my grandmother, fine seaming was a proper
and prideful thing . . . weaving well-nigh invisible stitches
in and out with her shiny needle pushed
by Great-grandmother's silver thimble
(I never could master it—I still stick my fingers).
"Bettie Cosby, do be still! Ladies don't whistle."
That first piece cowers in shame in the brass-bound trunk,
that awful pink butterfly worn out
with eight-year-old mistakes done and re-done
and *done* again.
Sometimes I look back with no small compassion
on that poorest-excuse-for-a-girlchild.

A TRUE YARD BY THE NOSE

Growing up, I used to think
she smelled the inches in a yard
of calico
stretched from fingertip to nose.
The salt cupped grainy in her palm
a miracle, gauged from flesh
that knew from years
how half a teaspoon felt.
A dash of this,
a lump of that—
a pinch of soda
between forefinger and thumb,
enough to raise the biscuits
high and light.
Grandmother taught me to sew and cook
with a measuring tape and graduated spoons,
but they rest idle in a drawer—
my nose has learned to smell
as true a yard as hers.

COUNTRY WATCH DOGS

I.

Guineas make the best watch dogs.
A dark cacophony of pot-rack pot-rack
squawked in the night
at anything that moves or breathes—
enough to scare the bravest prowler
white-eyed.
We hunted their eggs,
speckled in fence corners,
and stuck discarded feathers
in our hair
at war-whoop angles.

II.

Rex was fierce.
Once owned by a city man
who taught him such snarls
even his owner was afraid
to come home,
he was banished to the farm
and growled tenderly
with babies crawling on his back
and tail pulling.
But the hens were suddenly safe,
and straying neighbors
went around by the other road.
Rex died on Highway 16.
He came up from the gulley
through high weeds
to follow us to the creek.

ON A COLD WINTER'S NIGHT

Delicate and fresh,
that first taste of November meat
killed when nights grew cold enough
to hold a carcass.
By deep-freeze time, dried peas
and cornbread had lost their charm;
and greens from the fall garden
cooked with chunks of salt pork
were just something to eat.
No sooner had the fattened pig
been hung, scraped clean and pink,
from the 2 x 4 on the side of the shed
than Mama made us a feast:
brains scrambled with eggs
and hot biscuits bubbly with butter
and dark thick sorghum from the syrup mill.
The next week would bring
liver with onions,
tongue with mustard sauce,
fresh loin with cream gravy—
but never anything so good
as that first sweet bite
of winter's meat.

LYE SOAP AND DIRIGIBLES

One Monday morning during the short years
at Shoal Creek, the Goodyear blimp came
to hover a day's excitement
over Spalding County, looking
for all the world like the pig bladder
blown up for a country game of ball.
I saw it first—to great danger
of bashing my head with the windlass
of the deep well in the front yard.
It was wash day and a million buckets
of cold water had to come up
from a hundred feet straight down
toward China . . . and I was IT, Mama's chief
assistant and water-drawer. Bill, being next
in size, brought wood to feed the hungry fire
under the black iron pot bubbling
with overalls, underwear, and strong lye soap
made in winter at hog-killing time.
I drew water all morning, grinding out curses
on the windlass at that blimp floating
sassy as a white summer cloud
without a single lick of work to do.

INDIAN SPRINGS

Grandmother had unshaken faith
in the sulphur water that boiled out
into the fieldstone box at Indian Springs.
She brought it home in demi-johns
that stood milky-green in the pantry
to be drunk three times a day
as therapy for kidneys, gall bladders
(and gout too, I guess).
She made us drink some once in a while,
but failed to appreciate our humor
when we held our noses and said it tasted
like dead Indians mixed with rotten eggs.
Not that Indian Springs didn't have charms . . .
it was a great place for class picnics
with a wide shallow stream and slippery rocks
(no fun at all if somebody didn't fall in).
Only thing, nobody had much appetite there
for deviled eggs, so nobody ever brought any.

ODE FOR A NEW BROTHER

Another brother, George this time,
and him forever tied to Sister and me
being sent across the state
to Aunt Etta's with Alophen pills
for homesick digestion, and chewing
one up with a soda cracker
into an odious mess.
They had Lincoln Logs
and a cold clean Methodist parlor
not very friendly when cock's crow
at Shoal Creek waked me too early.
Hand-me-down shorts from Cousin Edna
(with bloomers inside).
I cut them out with her scissors—
a wicked ungrateful thing to have done,
but we didn't really need
another brother anyway.

HAM AND EGG PIE

Summers, my favorite place to go was Uncle Harry's,
over in the country past Union City and Sharpsburg,
all the windows of the old touring car wide open
to blow out the smoke of Dad's cigars (winter visiting
stank—thick acrid fumes shut up with five squabbling
kids and a half-grown hound pup or two
that Dad was taking to his favorite brother).
Next to Grandma, Aunt Cora was the best cook—
once she baked six kinds of pie
for a family gathering, and the black ants
got in the piesafe overnight.
You would have thought the last trump
of judgment had come, the way she raved.
She was somewhat mollified by the other aunts'
reassurance that Fanny Farmer herself
had never made lighter pie crust
or tastier gravy to float the tender bits
of home-cured ham and plump yellow eggs.
It took the whole gaggle of cousins
to find all the eggs on Uncle Harry's farm—
country hens hide in the barn loft
in curly nests of hay, or in the rump-curved
hayrake seat on a folded croker sack.
We felt important, finding eggs. Ones we didn't
the hounds would, and if there was anything
the Mixon men despised, it was an egg-sucking
dog.

I must have heard a hundred times
how Uncle Harry developed
his fondness for eggs:
hungry in France during the Great War,
he found a nest behind a bombed-out farmhouse
and scrambled the whole dozen
in his helmet
over a fire of appletree twigs.

THE SAD HISTORY OF AN INNOCENT VICTIM

The hieroglyphics on my knees
scribble a reminder that Bill pushed me
down in the tool shed on a pile of roofing nails;
the white line on my lip (only shows when I'm mad),
that he threw a teaspoon at Sister. She ducked . . .
cut me through to the teeth.
On my right leg, the souvenir of a fencing match—
long sticks heated to smoldering under the washpot
one gallant Monday. The other leg? A pair of scissors
that missed their mark . . . she ducked again.
If this implies that Bill was the villain of the piece,
catch him sometime when the chores are done
and he's holding a pole over the catfish pond—
maybe he'll show you *his* scars.

SET AND SING 'TIL TWELVE O' CLOCK

Counting out is a ritual
as old as when children play.
Mama knows the rhymes
and her mother
and her mother's mother's mother
over in Jones County.
You don't learn the words,
you just know them
when time comes for choosing up
teams down in the pasture
or behind the school.
   William, William, Trembletoe,
   He's a good fisherman; he has hens.
   Some lay eggs, some lay none.
   Wire, brier, limberlock,
   Set and sing 'til twelve o'clock.
   O-U-T spells OUT,
   You old dirty dishrag dog.
Charlie is one captain
(he has the ball),
and Dorothy the other
(she owns the jump rope).
They fight over the ones
who can run fastest,
but nobody wants the little ones
(they don't do anything
but skin their knees).

Bobby can't bat, and cries
when Charlie doesn't want her
on his team. I can't bat
or run fast either . . .
but I *won't* cry.

A LIBERAL EDUCATION

The pacing vet is ten, his assistant
a four year old in red overalls.
Expert, they watch with clinical interest
the every push of the tan and white calf
that emerges to stand wobbly and wet
in the barn lot. A pat on the horn
for brave Sally, a word to her offspring,
and the old hands swagger off to inspect
their previous triumph, a litter of calicos
ready to open their eyes in the barn loft.
The propagation of the race is no mystery
to the proud owners of a 4-H project
and an old mother cat in the barn.

SEE THE LITTLE PUFFA-BILLIES ALL IN A ROW

Down at the station, early in the morning,
See the little puffa-billies all in a row.
See the engine driver turn a little handle,
Puff Puff Chug Chug! Off they go!

For Shoal Creek kids
miles from plane, train, bus
(a car we had—an old Model T),
seeing the train was the Fourth of July
and Halloween rolled into one.
The trestle on Taylor St.
was just three blocks from Grandmother's house
and on the safe side of Highway 41 too.
When the pleasures of the joggling board
and the bronze sundial
marking time in the back garden
had palled,
we shimmied through the privet hedge
and up the alley to the railroad bridge,
hanging our country faces over
as far as danger
to see the engineer's striped cap
and return his cheery wave.
The faraway places on boxcar doors:
NC&StL, GREAT NORTHERN,
and UNION PACIFIC in blue and white letters
rolled us out to Zane Grey's West,

cowboys and Indians on clacking wheels
that faded off across the highway
and right on down to the county line.

CLIMB—TO THE SLENDEREST TWIG

And the two of us, Bill and me,
hoisting our baby sister fifty feet
(or was it a hundred?)
up into the eyrie
of our twin trees down by the creek
(said magnificent height being gained
by a most ingenious inching
of bare feet and overalled bottoms
pressed between opposite sides of the bark-rough dare).
Once higher than the ridgepole of the big barn,
we shouted our success into the footloose winds
of vacation,
jubilant until a small and fretful voice,
hardly daring to ask:
"Sister, I gotta go . . .
how are you going to get me down . . . quick?"
And Dad
hurrying across the pasture
with his tallest ladder
and . . . pausing . . .
to break one slight but supple peachtree limb
just big enough to sting.

AMONG THE RED BALLOONS

We float among the red balloons,
as young as the first circus day
we held Grandfather's hand
to the open field at the edge of town.
With tents and brave flags,
elephants and pretty ladies on white horses,
he was forever six and we
would never grow older.
Gone was the ticker tape,
gone the cotton market and Mr. Combs
writing behind the tall brown desk
on Taylor St.
Gone too the neat blue suit,
disappeared behind a clown's mask—
grinning,
with sawdust in his thin gray hair.

NO PRAYER FOR SISTER

She was going to die like Beth
in *Little Women,* and it was all our fault.
Bill and I huddled in the barn loft,
the sweet alfalfa hay for once no consolation.
We were supposed to look after her,
and we had let her fall, crack her head
sharp on the 2 x 4 in the back yard.
We didn't think it would hurt
to let her walk the big oil drum—
she could skin-the-cat in the peachtree
and walk the barn rafters.
Now she was lying in the back room,
face as white as Mama's—
and Dad off in the field somewhere.
We were scared to ask for a miracle,
we didn't deserve one.
And by the time she came to,
we didn't need a whipping.

INDIAN CORN

We played at Creeks and Cherokees,
found arrowheads and potsherds in plum thickets
where the Indians used to plant grains
like yellow fingernails in sandy bottomland
where the river bent to meet the creek.
The flowing waters marked the passing
of ancient seasons when thin white parings
uncurled into waving leaves and golden silks.
Corn grew taller there than the nut-brown
children, and stored up meal for winter
when summer's berries had been pressed and dried,
and hickory smoke rose lazy from deerskin lodges
like the river mist on a warm vacation morning.

CAMP MEETING

There's power in the blood
and August floored with sawdust,
slab-sided shingled tents
and second-best dishes brought
in cardboard boxes sweet
with pound cakes and boiled custard.
The tinny piano, hoarse
from a year's disuse,
leads the choir
fervent in print dresses
cooled with Pittman's Funeral Home fans.
The old talk old times:
how Grandpa prayed all night
over the town drunkard
and converted him
to Sam Jones, a mighty preacher.
The young run fast games of tag,
hurrying up the years
until they're old enough
to meet in shy pairs
and hold hands on the last bench.
Across the dirt road,
the family graves lie
blanketed brown

with last year's pine needles
where early spring will push up green
with daffodils.

COUNTRY STORE

Sometime during the lean years
when the mortgage hung like a thunder cloud
over Septembers, Dad put up a little store
on the highway. Those of us big enough
to make change sold crackers and sardines,
gas and sacks of chicken feed
afternoons after school and on Saturdays.
One of our customers was Plunk Holland—
he lived across the creek on the Rogers' place,
patriarch in a broom-swept yard
swarming with cafe au lait children
of no special parentage.
We rather envied them—they didn't have to
go to school, and ate fried bologna
for breakfast (we had oatmeal and toast
morning after nourishing morning).
The none-too-sober Plunk and his harem
bought "on a credit, pay you Sad'dy"—
flat cans of Mme. Melba's Hair Straightener,
and large size Sweet Shrub Snuff
with bonus coupons.
And bologna.

STAR LIGHT, STAR BRIGHT

Standing on the edge of the farm's faint glow,
I spoke my secrets to the dark country sky.
Hailing that great inconceivable distance,
jubilant with tiny winking lights,
I almost believed that I could charm one
to my hands, rub it like a genie's lamp
and see my wishes appear, suddenly shimmering,
jeweled out of the night.

GREEK GODS AND CALICO CATS

A high-spirited stallion stalked our back pasture,
disdainful among the lowly mules.
He pulled the plow with much head-tossing,
carefully stepping on more cotton than he missed.
We were positive that Hercules was a racehorse
before his station fell to the plow—
maybe even ran in that Kentucky Derby
we sometimes heard on the squawky radio.
We named him for that hero well met
in Mr. Hawthorne's *Tanglewood Tales*
read by Mama around the wood stove on winter nights.
Our nodding acquaintance with the Greeks
lent a decidedly non-country air
to the animals at Shoal Creek.
Jason and Medea, the barn cats, stalked
their Golden Fleece among the feed sacks in the hayloft,
kingly with nine lives, mice, and milk squirted fresh
in their bowl when Dad milked Bess and Lou.
Jason took an unscheduled trip to Olympus
under the iron heel of Hercules,
but Medea went on to found a dynasty of calicos
as speckled as the dominecker hen and James—
he lived behind us on the Cartledge place
and you couldn't put a pin on him
without stabbing a freckle.

I used to wonder if he was freckled
under his overalls—
I found out for sure one July afternoon
at the swimming hole by Double Sewers.

THE CURSE

Growing up was more than we had bargained for.
The hard way: Ethel, working a thorny problem
in arithmetic at the board
with a great spot spreading
on her pale yellow skirt.
Miss Emma read curiosity and horror
in watching eyes, and hurried Ethel home.
Poor Ethel! She could Charleston like nobody
you ever saw—loose-limbed as a rag doll
and twice as agile.
Miss Amy told us how she had tried to wash
"it" away in a tub of cold water—
her lady mother having been too delicate
to discuss such matters with a child.
Later, we had Miss Betty in the Home Ec. room.
She told us the facts and dispensed spirits
of ammonia and comfort with a sympathetic face
freckled under wild red hair. She dried my tears
the day I threw up in Coach's class.
I had always liked Math before that.

THE MIXED PERFUMES OF CHILDHOOD

Ink on my pigtails—
Billy dipped them in,
sixth grade, I think it was.
And that awful "Blue Waltz" toilet water
that Cousin Lena wore—
10 cents a bottle, and it made me sneeze.
Spring rain and mud puddles,
warm to my ankles and soft between my toes
that awful day I broke out with chicken pox
right in the middle of wading.
Mama was horrified (thought I was gonna die).
Such an unclean disease, and such a rotty smell!
The attic was best—
and rummaging in Great-grandmother's trunk:
mothballs in the pockets
of Grandpa's Confederate uniform,
and rose petals browned between the staining folds
of Mamie's wedding dress.

A GOOD RUN OF KRAUT

"Signs are right for a run of kraut,
the sun's right, moon's right,
everything's right."
And the great heads of cabbage grew
plump and round,
leaved like green roses
to slice paper-thin
and salt down in crocks
with clean smooth stones
to hold the lids in place.
I hated chopping kraut—
never could do it
without chopping my fingers too.

APPRECIATION OF THE ARTS

We had "The Man with the Hoe"
black and white on the third grade wall,
and "The Blue Boy" bright on the cover
of a calendar that came with two boxes
of Cloverine Salve.
When I was eight I memorized
Joaquim Miller's "Columbus"
and went around for months reciting
"Sail on, Sail on and on . . ."
until practically everybody
in the neighborhood (and Orrs Elementary)
wished that America had never been found.
But best of all was the old Edison
in the front hall. We fought for
the privilege of cranking up its
wheezy insides, and choosing a thick black disc
of Mme. Schumann-Heink warbling away
in German, Caruso's faraway voice
in the Pagliacci, and two whole records
(front and back) of how somebody seduced
somebody else in "Cavalleria Rusticana."
We hadn't the foggiest notion what
it all meant—but it did liven up a rainy
afternoon when thunder had drowned out
the chorus of tree toads rehearsing
in the alder bushes down behind the barn.

QUILTIN' BEE

Today I buy blankets of acrylic fibers
without a history, made on humming machines
that I have never seen . . .
but their touch is not warm with neighbors' voices,
stick cats, and Mama's best print dresses.
"Star of Texas" and "Step Around the Mountain"—
patterns passed down from Grandmother's time,
hoarded and treasured like recipes for a Lane cake
or light soda biscuits.
Tales told by neighbor women,
gathered in the spare room around the quiltin' frame:
the Wog dark in the meadow of a full-moon night,
how Tanny Boggus chased Sally Ann down by the creek.
Each one signed her section in tiny prideful stitches—
Mamie Jones quilted a three-finger-size cat
to prove her skill (like my stick figures
drawn in Shoal Creek's sandy edge).
I finger a soft square from Papa's velour coat,
golden and furry as my kitten;
a blue piece from Mama's meeting dress,
a square from Sister's Sunday apron—
and I ponder the unfamiliar ones.
Who wore these brightly patterned scraps
my fingers do not know?

PEANUT BUTTER AND TADPOLE CAKES

Some of our cousins from town thought
we really ate fat cakes of brown creek mud—
we even had them believing the tadpoles
we caught and used for eyes and noses
were a rare treat. The whipping of the
year came from convincing the smallest one
to eat a "peanut butter cake with raisins."
Mama never could get Sam to eat another bite
at out house, even our favorite sandwich:
peanut butter spread thick and dotted with raisins
laid on in elaborate patterns and mashed down . . .
hard . . . until it squished up like fresh mud
between toes spring-free as tadpoles
wriggling in a muddy muddy pool.

IF YOU DON'T JUMP, YOU'RE A SISSY

A superb moment of bravado . . .
leaping into the vacation air
from the loft-perch of the old chicken house,
spurred into reckless action
by a swaggering younger brother
already twice master of the feat.
Now, when alarming seat belts are fastened
and the "no-smoking" light cautions yellow,
I help the 747 rev its powerful engines
and fortify myself to plummet again.
My feet search in panic
for the assurance of solid floor . . .
as Icarus, flimsy feathers and all,
venturing toward a Cretan promontory;
the Brothers Montgolfier
guiding their fragile linen globe
above the staring crowds at Annonay;
and Alan Shepard aiming a porcelain nose-cone
toward the soft mattress
of chicken wire rolled in the barnyard.

CHILDHOOD IN BLACK AND WHITE

Cleaning lamp globes.
Nasty black sooty things!
No soap could cut the greasy
black glop . . . but you're the oldest,
it's your job. YUK!
Come, butter, come.
Come, butter, come.
Nasty chant to stroke the nasty dasher
in the nasty milk.
Too warm!
Too cold!
CHURN, CHURN, CHURN!
One night, rocking by the fire,
lamp and churn too close.
Milk and glass all over the floor.
That darned churnful won't
COME, BUTTER, COME!

BILL'S FIRST HAIRCUT

Grandmother Cosby was a tiger.
If there were no fair means,
she resorted to foul.
She thought Bill's curls were unmanly,
Dad refused to have them cut.
Grandmother schemed—
deliciously-underhanded plot.
Gently, she filled innocent ears
with tales of round-pointed scissors
and cutting of hair,
for Christmas, a brightly-wrapped book
of paper soldiers with shiny new cutters
rounded safe for little fingers.
He did it Christmas night,
right up through the curl
in the middle of his forehead!
Grandmother, smiling to herself no doubt,
calmly scooped up the ragged lamb
and took him to the barber.
Poor Dad,
he was no match for a tiger.

ON OLD BLOODSTAINS

Robert was legend, knight, and moral
of Grandmother's back garden:
Don't climb on the scuppernong arbor,
remember—Robert did—
and fell on the knife-sharp sundial!
We saw the blood running fresh on our grass,
the young belly torn,
heard sirens screaming . . .
a powerful vision to keep greedy children
from sweet brown grapes just beyond tip-toe.
To meet him was bitter treachery—
no pale hero, this gray man!
Only old blood congealed in the crevices
of the sundial's bronze blade.

LILLIE BELLE*

*Everybody has another grandmother—
someday I'll write a book especially
for Lillie Belle who lived across the state
and another creek ran past her door.

Grandmother, sorceress of the wood stove—
charming a scrawny old yard rooster
into such a tender dumplinged dish
that my hand was slapped
for daring a finger
run around the bowl
to capture the one last gravy drop.
She learned survival tactics
feeding thirteen
on the dubious bounty
of an upland farm—
red clay caked around puny cornstalks
yielding punier ears.
The peach tree in the back yard
hung with wormy knotty fruit—
but enchanted by Grandmother's knife,
they made a golden gleam
in Mason jars on the pantry shelf,
and peach pies cooling
in the piesafe with pricked tin doors.
And marmalade.

FOR GEORGE, AFTER TWENTY YEARS

Too soon I watched you die. Too young
to understand your arching body suddenly relaxed.
I shouted worn-out parents to see you well again,
miraculously at rest from writhing days.
(Why do you lie so still
in your white linen suit?)
Over and over, I watched you die
each time I closed my eyes against another child
too deep asleep for me to reach by shouting—
my child this time, but imaged in a brother's face
nightmares could not forget.
But *she* woke.
At last you may lie quiet.
She walks, halting, but she walks.
In blue pajamas new for celebration.

PARKING LOT ON TAYLOR STREET

I walk across the concrete
to the new A & P.
Every step crushes my memory
of green grass, larkspur,
and ragged robins
around the bronze sundial
shadowing a summer afternoon.
And the wicker table is laid
with Grandmother's blue china tea
set on a white linen cloth
cross-stitched with roses.
In my cupboard, one saucer, two cups—
all that remains of a thousand tea parties,
tiny cakes and sandwiches
miraculously appearing
through the latticed door
with William in his starched white coat.

SEND ME FOUR BALLOONS FOR MY BIRTHDAY

Green for kudzu vines shading a porch swing
on a red clay hill
and turnip greens bubbling
in the big pot with two handles
that Mama cooked oatmeal and raisins in.
Pink for soft red hair
and gingham aprons belted for a small brother
when brothers were mostly something to fight with
and this one a breathing toy.
Blue for a length of broadcloth
on my birthday
when Depression made Dad's pockets tight
and his fists closed hard around 39 cents a yard.
White for a linen suit with short pants,
satin to line a small coffin.
and icing for a chocolate cake
at the party we didn't have.

CURSES

When we were young and mad at Mama,
we swore we would go out in the garden and eat worms:
long slimy, slimmy worms big fat juicy worms
little bitty fuzzy-wuzzy worms.
Worms were tame fare—not likely to bring forth
the washing-out-of-mouth with Octagon soap
that cleaned up a slipped-out "damn!"
"Great Caeser's Ghost!" was safe, and "Napoleon
Bonaparte's Britches!"—just so long as Mama
pretended not to know they stood for "bad" words.
After George died, the rest of us didn't say ugly
things around Mama—it made her cry because she
washed one of our words out of his mouth
the week before he died.

"CHRISTMAS GIFT!"

She called from the open door,
grinning all over to be first with the greeting.
"Christmas Gift!" we shouted, glad to be beaten
by such a laughing grandmother.
Traditional, this start of holiday joy—
cousins wriggling with excitement
for presents, and pumpkin pie spicy and brown,
turkey dressing and groaning on the bench
in the front hall until the lovely pain
wore off.
The hall is gone where one Christmas afternoon
I woke and tried to fly, from dreams of angels
and partridges in pear trees—but I still make
her pumpkin pie. This year when I "Christmas Gift!"
my first grandchild, Grandmother will smile somewhere
to see me stand in the open door of another house,
trying to fill her place.

QUINTUPLETS FOR SISTER

They were all she asked:
the Dionnes had been born that year
and dolls in fives filled every shop
in town, $10.00 the set. But Santa had only
$10.00, and the five of us to gift.
Necessity invented—the dimestore
had babies 29 cents a piece,
with no clothes on. Mama didn't like
to sew but sew by night she did—
five flannel gowns
and five pink rosebud blankets bound in blue.
Sister loved them for years, never knowing
that her babies weren't the patented,
authenticated, genuine Dionnes.

NIGHTHAWKS IN A SUMMER SKY

> *Bullbat, bullbat,*
> *come and get your wool hat!*
> *Bullbat, bullbat,*
> *come and get your wool hat!*

I remember a tow-headed row
chanting on a poplar limb,
willing bare feet, brown arms
to feather and carry them
high over Hollow Chestnut Gap
into the orange lands,
the fabulous lands
where the setting sun goes
to see dragon kites rise
and hear slant-eyed children sing.

WHEN I CONSIDER MY FATHER, DEAD THREE YEARS

He was a hard man,
close-mouthed with Depression
and the feeding of us in hard times.
He scarcely spoke when mortgages pressed
his temples and one great purple vein
throbbed in tempo to the pain.
We thought he was mad at us.

Yet I carry another snapshot—
face smoothed somehow with years,
the great vein quieted and slow.
A ragged pith helmet shades
his farm-tanned cheeks
and the stump of a King Edward cigar
moves with the mouth that talked
to me (booted feet on the porch rail)—
of politics and race, grandchildren
and the price of corn.
Only then did I begin to know
the hard man
I have almost forgotten.

OF SUNDAY AFTERNOONS

White figures on a brass bedstead,
and I once daring to put my eye
(stooping only a little, being small)
to the knothole low in the backroom door.
They never knew I carried the image
back into the dusty Sunday yard
and up a peach tree to hold.
It was knowledge too deep to share,
forbidden secret that somehow warmed
my days at Shoal Creek.
The knothole is now too low—
only my heart can bend to remember
such love as joined them
for fifty years and more
to lie among the weaving pine roots
in Mt. Zion churchyard.

REQUIEM FOR CONRAD

Once upon a childhood was enough
to have my breath knocked out—
to lie between the rows, gasping,
while Hercules, wicked hooves printed
purple on my belly,
munched on Dad's precious corn.
Once, more than enough
for my brother's friend Conrad.
He frowns out of a fourth grade
school picture, forever ten
by virtue of a balky mule.

MY LAST RIDE

Four on Hercules,
big sister
bringing up the wide rear.
Hercules going his way
around the corner of the barn—
Whoa!
and under the low 2 x 4
for hanging fat pink pigs
at the first cold snap
of November. Whoa!
And scraping (as clean
as any pig) the broad back
free of children.
Underneath, the drag harrow
with gaping iron teeth
raised up for a winter's rest,
and purple bruises
for the brave rear guard.

FOR REBECCA, WITH TEMPERED SADNESS

Across from Mt. Zion, pine needles
on red clay gashed last year for him.
A space beside for her, unconscious
waiting for a brown hand to smooth
her cheek as if to say that fifty years
were few, that she was fair.
    Smells of meat loaf,
    strange potato salad—
    neighbor's best cooking,
    names taped on dishes.
Eleven months they slept apart,
this gentle pair who made me
first born, when they had no more
lines on their faces
than a wedding picture gold-framed.
A pine needle falls like a brown scratch
on a blanket of white chrysanthemums,
The pines are impatient to cover the earth.
    Is it pumpkin pie
    or Miss Martha's famous potato?
My brother has a scrap of paper
in his hand. He has written:
Earth heals sooner than the heart.
    Paper plates of pie,
    tea in paper cups.
    Was it pumpkin?

Two sisters watch with linen handkerchiefs.
There were three little girls
with stiff sausage curls and high-buttoned shoes
in the picture on Grandmother's mantelpiece.
   Hot and black in paper cups—
   coffee is good with the pie.
Grandsons cleared the thicket last year,
now, taller, they have cleared again.
We will plant daffodils.
They will go to a football game
in Jacksonville and cheer the team.
   Definitely pumpkin.

First prize, the Shel McDonald Dramatic Poetry Award,
1977, the National Federation of State Poetry Societies.

THE PATCHWORK COAT

She wore the coat to comings out,
and proms with lemonade
pink under Japanese lanterns
flickering in dark back yards.
And tossed it over a favorite
dancing dress,
a watered silk cotillion dress
that waltzed
across the parquet floors.

Eighty now, she wears the coat,
hugging old bones warm in memories
of a lady turned sixteen.
Her mother pieced the patterns then,
featherstitched each random square,
lined it soft with scarlet silk
the year Marie put her hair up high
with gutta-percha pins.

There are scraps of Papa's paisley tie
that matched his best blue suit
(saved for funerals and such),
and bits from Etta's wedding dress,
wild roses white brocaded,

that rustled down the aisle
to organ notes that swell again
when wrinkled fingers stroke
the yellowing threads.

ACKNOWLEDGMENTS

DeKalb Literary Arts Journal
Country Store
Camp Meeting
Gypsies and Water Moccasins
Fire at Night

College English
On Old Bloodstains

The Tattler
The Mixed Perfumes of Childhood

The Unicorn
Quintuplets for Sister

The Yearbook of Modern Poetry '76
Ode for a New Brother

Descant
Indian Corn

Poem 28
The Day Dick and Jane Bit the Dust

Ball State Forum
No Prayer for Sister
By Shoal Creek

America
Mag
Clean Rags and Kerosene

Niagara Magazine
Laney

Nitty-Gritty
See the Little Puffa-billies All in a Row
Set and Sing 'til Twelve O' Clock

Bardic Echoes
A Poor Excuse for a Girlchild

The Sunstone Review
When I Consider My Father, Dead Three Years